NNAT®2 Practice Test – Level D

Illustrations by: Kenneth Sommer
Written and published by: Bright Kids NYC

Corporate Headquarters:
Bright Kids NYC
225 Broadway, Suite 1504
New York, NY 10007
www.brightkidsnyc.com
info@brightkidsnyc.com
917-539-4575

About Bright Kids NYC

Bright Kids NYC was founded in New York City to provide language arts and math enrichment for young children and to educate parents about standardized tests through workshops and consultations, as well as to prepare young children for such tests though assessments, tutoring, and publications. Our philosophy is that regardless of age, test-taking is a skill than can be acquired and mastered through practice.

At Bright Kids NYC, we strive to provide the best learning materials. Our publications are truly unique. First, all of our books have been created by qualified psychologists, learning specialists, and teachers. Second, our books have been tested by hundreds of children in our tutoring practice. Since children can make associations that many adults cannot, testing of materials by children is critical to creating successful test preparation guides. Finally, our learning specialists and teaching staff have provided practical strategies and tips so parents can best help their child prepare to compete successfully on standardized tests.

Feel free to contact us should you have any questions.

Corporate Headquarters:
Bright Kids NYC
225 Broadway, Suite 1504
New York, NY 10007
www.brightkidsnyc.com
info@brightkidsnyc.com
917-539-4575

Introduction

Bright Kids NYC created the NNAT®2 Practice Test to familiarize children with the content and the format of the NNAT®2. Children, no matter how bright they are, do not always perform well when they are not accustomed to the format and the structure of a test. Children can misunderstand the directions, fail to consider all the answer choices, and may not always read the questions carefully. Thus, without adequate preparation and familiarization, children may not always perform to the best of their ability on standardized tests such as the NNAT®2.

This Bright Kids NNAT®2 Practice Test is not designed to generate a score or a percentile rank as the test has not been standardized with the actual NNAT®2 norms and standards. The objective of the practice test is to identify your child's strengths, weaknesses, and overall test-taking ability so that you can prepare your child adequately for the actual test.

In order to maximize the effectiveness of the Bright Kids NNAT®2 Practice Test, it is important to first familiarize yourself with the test and its instructions. In addition, it is recommended that you designate a quiet place to work with your child, ideally in a neutral environment free of noise and clutter. Finally, provide a comfortable and proper seating arrangement to enable your child to focus and concentrate to the best of his or her ability.

Children will be taking many standardized tests throughout their school years. Teaching your child critical thinking skills along with test-taking strategies at a young age will benefit your child for many years to come. Our philosophy is that regardless of age, test-taking is a skill that can be acquired and mastered through practice.

NNAT®2 Overview

The *Naglieri Nonverbal Ability Test* – Second Edition (NNAT®2) is designed to provide a nonverbal measure of general ability. NNAT®2 items do not require the student to read, write, or speak, so students must rely on reasoning, as opposed to verbal skills, to solve the problems presented to them. The NNAT®2 is appropriate for use with diverse populations of students since the geometric shapes used in NNAT®2 are universal and the test is completely nonverbal. The NNAT®2 is a revision and an updated version of the *Naglieri Nonverbal Ability Test – Multilevel Form* (NNAT-ML; Naglieri, 1997).

All of the information needed to solve each NNAT®2 problem is presented in the item. For example, one figural matrix format requires a student to identify what is missing in a pattern.

Figure 1: Sample NNAT®2 Question

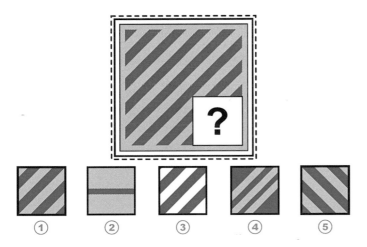

NNAT®2 scores provide an estimate of the student's ability based on the number of test questions answered correctly compared to other students of the same age. The NNAT®2 can be administered in a group or online, on a computer.

NNAT®2 is a timed test, and students have 30 minutes to complete 48 questions.

NNAT®2 – Level D

NNAT®2 Content

The NNAT®2 is a nonverbal measure of general ability that is designed specifically to predict academic success. The student must examine the relationships among the parts of a matrix and determine the correct response based on the information provided within the matrix. Students must pick the correct response from five possible answer choices.

The NNAT®2 test consists of the following four different types of questions:

1. Pattern Completion

The first question type requires the student to find the correct piece that completes a pattern. These types of items typically appear more at the Elementary Level NNAT®2 tests since they are among the easiest of the matrix items.

Figure 2: Pattern Completion Example

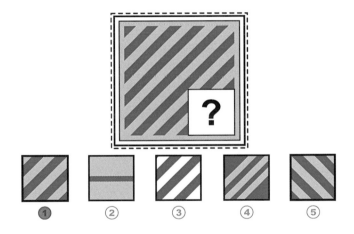

2. Reasoning by Analogy

The second type of question requires the student to recognize a logical relationship between several geometric shapes to find the right answer. The student must see how an object changes as it appears in the squares across the rows and down the columns of the matrix. The student must see how the shapes change throughout the matrix and be able to simultaneously work with more than one change such as shape and rotation. These items increase in difficulty when multiple changes occur across rows and columns.

Figure 3: Analogy Example

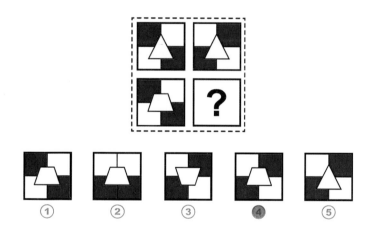

3. Serial Reasoning

A third type of question requires the student to recognize the sequence of shapes and how the sequence changes across the rows and columns. In this type of a question, shapes change across the row, and within the columns, throughout the item. For example, as each shape appears in a row, it also appears one position to the right, creating a series of designs that change over the matrix. This type of a matrix becomes more difficult when multiple series are included in the matrix.

Figure 4: Series Example

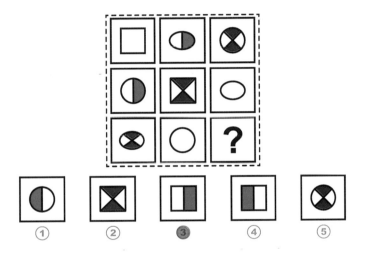

4. Spatial Visualization

The fourth type of question requires the student to recognize how multiple designs would look if combined. The student has to find the answer by adding the images in the boxes above or to the left of the empty box and determine what the final image would look like if the elements are combined. These types of questions are more complex, since they involve rotations or shapes intersecting in ways that could be difficult to visualize.

Figure 5: Spatial Visualization Example

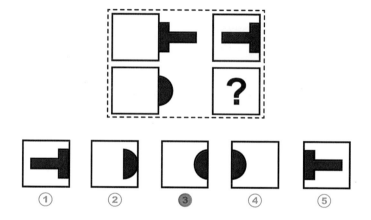

NNAT®2 Test Structure

The NNAT®2 is organized into seven levels, A through G, designed for students between Kindergarten and grade 12. It contains 48 items for students at each level for which the test is intended. There are three unique levels for each grade from Kindergarten through grade 2 due to the rapid growth in development in earlier grades. There is one level that is for both grades 3 and 4, and another level that is both for grades 5 and 6. The next level is appropriate for the middle school years and includes transition to high school (i.e. grades 7, 8, and 9), while the last level serves the last three high school grades (i.e. grades 10, 11, and 12). See the table below for the summary of NNAT®2 test levels and their corresponding grades.

Table 1: Summary of NNAT®2 Levels and Grades

Level	Grade(s)
A	K
B	1
C	2
D	3, 4
E	5, 6
F	7, 8, 9
G	10, 11, 12

NNAT®2 Scoring Guidelines

When it comes to the results of the NNAT®2 test, they comprise a wealth of useful information for test users. Derived scores based on age comparisons can be provided for all grade levels and the Naglieri Ability Index or NAI can be calculated for three-month intervals of chronological age to derive scaled scores. Raw score, which is defined as the number of questions answered correctly, does not provide enough information about the level of quality of student performance. However, the scaled score system connects all test levels and yields a continuous scale that can be used to compare the performance of students taking different levels of the same content cluster. Scaled scores are especially useful for comparing results from the same content cluster across levels, and for evaluating changes in performance over time. Scaled scores should be translated into percentile ranks and stanines in order to show the relative standings of a student in comparison to other students who are the same age.

The Bright Kids NNAT®2 Practice Test can be scored only based on total number of correct answers, or the overall raw score. Since this practice test has not been standardized with the NNAT®2 norms, scaled scores or percentile ranks cannot be obtained from the raw score. Please realize that a child can miss many questions on the test and still obtain a high score. Thus, it is important that this practice test be utilized as a learning tool to help evaluate a child's strengths and weaknesses, rather than to estimate a scaled score or a percentile rank.

NNAT®2 – Level D

How to Use this Book

This is a NNAT®2 Practice Test for Level D, which consists of 48 practice items along with an answer key.

Before you begin, it is important to familiarize yourself with the test and its instructions. Ideally, take the test yourself to ensure that you know how to solve the problems, should you need to review them with your child later. If your child gets frustrated, provide encouragement; even a simple sticker chart reward system can go a long way. Utilize the warm-up exercises provided to practice with your child to help him or her get comfortable with matching patterns. We have also included additional challenges at the end for those children who excel at this type of activity.

Once the test is complete, go over the questions and answers with your child. Ask him or her to verbalize what he or she sees so he or she can help find the right answer. Allow the child to construct his or her own matrices so that he or she understands how to solve them.

Please also review the following proven test-taking strategies to help your child succeed on the test:

1. **Listen to all the instructions.** It is important for children not to assume, but actually understand what is asked of them, including how to fill out the test forms. Make sure the child understands the instructions before he or she begins the test.

2. **Look at all the answer choices before choosing an answer.** Since no extra credit is given for finishing the test ahead of time, it is important for children to look at all answer choices carefully, before selecting a final answer.

3. **Use process of elimination to get to the right answer.** This is especially important if children are unsure of how to exactly solve the problem, but can intuitively deduct the answer from the answer choices available to them.

4. **If all else fails, take a guess.** Many children skip questions, but never have time to return to them. It is important to allocate a little time to make sure that all the questions have a marked answer, since there are no penalties for incorrect answers.

Getting Ready

Materials

1. Several No. 2 soft lead pencils, erasers, and pencil sharpeners.

2. Timer or a clock.

3. Ideally, a "Do Not Disturb" sign for the room where you will be administering the test.

Prior to Testing

1. Familiarize yourself with the test and the instructions. Take the actual test to make sure that you can later explain to the child why certain answers are correct or incorrect.

2. Provide satisfactory physical conditions in the room where the child will be taking the test. Make sure that there is ample lighting and ventilation.

3. To prevent interruptions, give the child the test when there are no other distractions in the house.

4. Complete the warm-up exercises prior to the test.

During Testing

1. Make sure that the child knows how to accurately mark the answers. Help the child as needed by utilizing the sample questions.

2. Do the sample questions together to make sure the child understands the instructions. Once the sample questions are complete, do not provide any more assistance. Discuss the answers only after the testing is complete.

3. Only allow 30 minutes for the child to complete the test.

Bright Kids NYC
NNAT®2 Practice Test

Warm-up Exercises

NNAT®2 – Level D

01 Match the patterns.

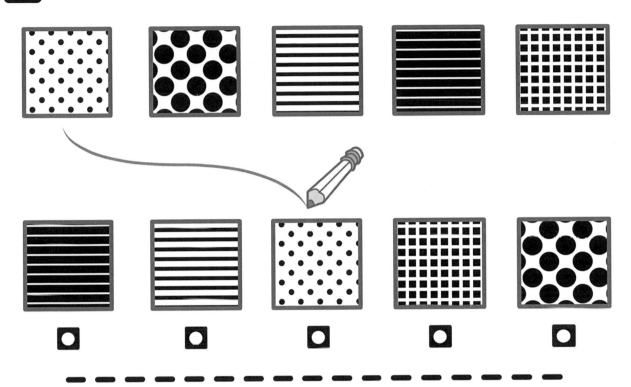

            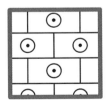

- -

02 Match the patterns.

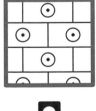   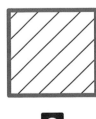      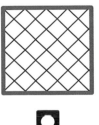   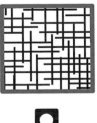

03 Match the patterns.

  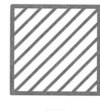  

- -

04 Match the patterns.

   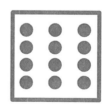 

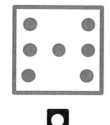 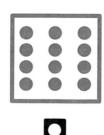 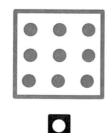 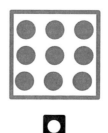 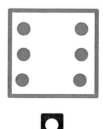

NNAT®2 – Level D   Bright Kids NYC Inc ©

05 Match the patterns.

- -

06 Match the patterns.

07 Match the patterns.

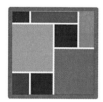    

○ ○ ○ ○ ○

- -

08 Match the patterns.

 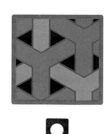   

○ ○ ○ ○ ○

NNAT®2 – Level D

09 Match the patterns.

   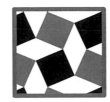 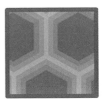

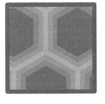    

○ ○ ○ ○ ○

- -

10 Match the patterns.

  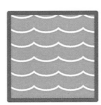  

   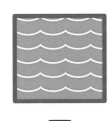 

○ ○ ○ ○ ○

NNAT®2 – Level D

Bright Kids NYC

NNAT®2 Practice Test

Questions
Level D
Grades 3 and 4

NNAT®2 – Level D

Sample Question Administration

SAY: **Today, we are going to do some fun activities. We will do the first three activities together.**

<u>SAMPLE ONE</u>

SAY: **Look at the picture below. There is something missing. Look at the answers below and find the piece that is missing.**

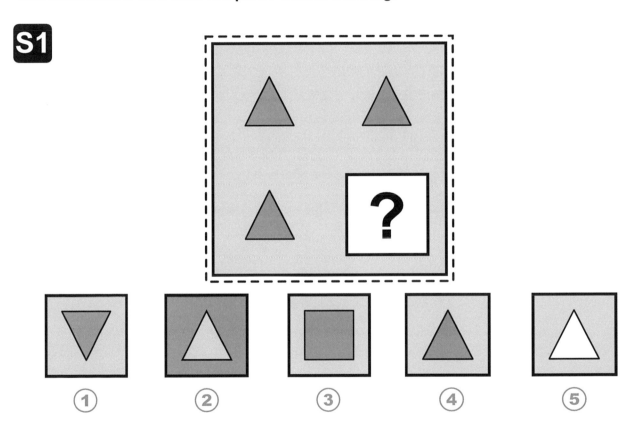

SAY: **Yes, the piece should be the orange triangle inside the blue box, which is number 4. Fill in the answer under the number 4, which is the correct answer.**

Demonstrate how to fill in an answer if the child seems confused. Remind the child that it does not have to be perfect, but circles must be visibly filled. Also let the child know that he or she can bubble only one answer choice. Proceed with the next sample question.

Answer the child's questions and make sure that he or she is comfortable with the answer choice.

SAMPLE TWO

SAY: **Look at the picture below. There is something missing. Look at the answers below and find the piece that is missing.**

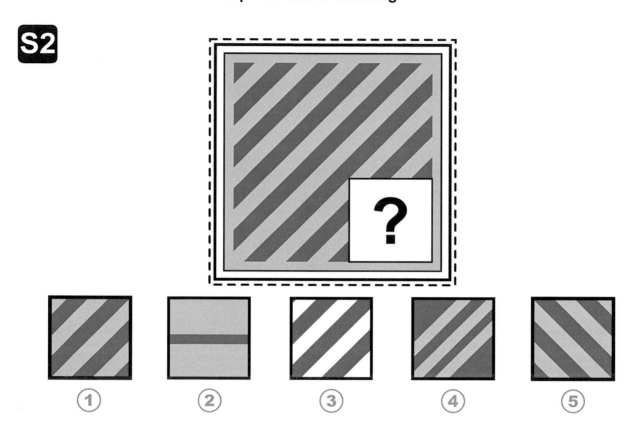

SAY: **Yes, the piece should be solid green with stripes, which is number 1. Fill in the answer under the number 1, which is the correct answer.**

Demonstrate how to fill in an answer if the child seems confused. Remind the child that it does not have to be perfect, but circles must be visibly filled. Also let the child know that he or she can bubble only one answer choice. Proceed with the next sample question.

Answer the child's questions and make sure that he or she is comfortable with the answer choice.

SAMPLE THREE

SAY: **Look at the picture below. There is something missing. Look at the answers below and find the piece that is missing.**

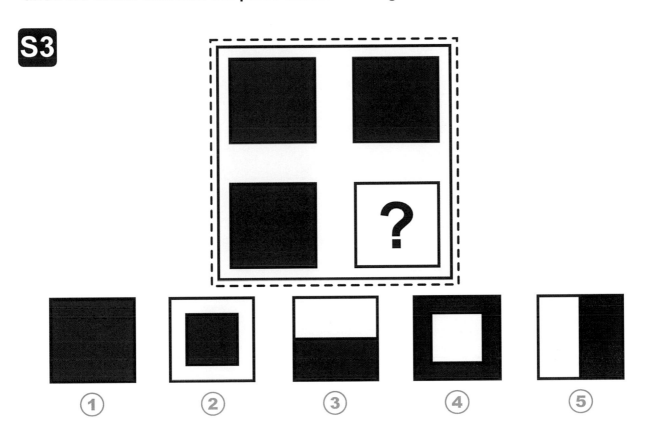

SAY: **Yes, the missing piece should be number 1. Fill in the answer under the number 1, which is the correct answer.**

Demonstrate how to fill in an answer if the child seems confused. Remind the child that it does not have to be perfect, but circles must be visibly filled. Also let the child know that he or she can bubble only one answer choice. Proceed with the next sample question.

Answer the child's questions and make sure that he or she is comfortable with the answer choice.

SAY: **On the next few pages, you will be doing more activities like these. Do the best that you can with each picture and do not worry if you are not sure of all of the answers. Be sure to bubble in the whole answer space each time you mark your answer. If you want to change an answer, erase all of your first mark and mark the new answer.**

Answer the child's questions before you move on to the actual test.

SAY: **Now turn the page and you may begin. I will let you know when to stop.**

Start timing and allow only 30 minutes to complete the test. After 30 minutes, complete the test.

01

①   ②   ③   ④   ⑤

02

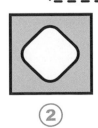  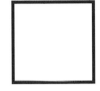  

①   ②   ③   ④   ⑤

03

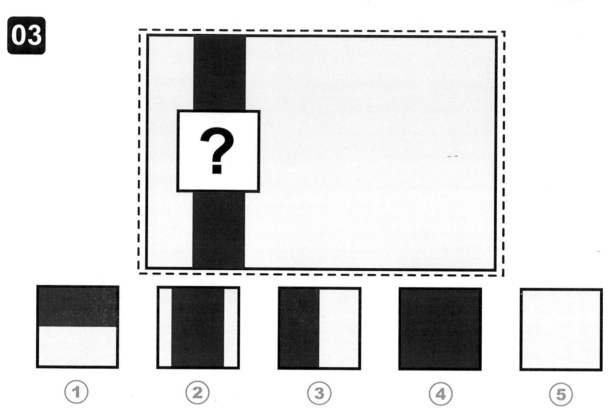

① ② ③ ④ ⑤

04

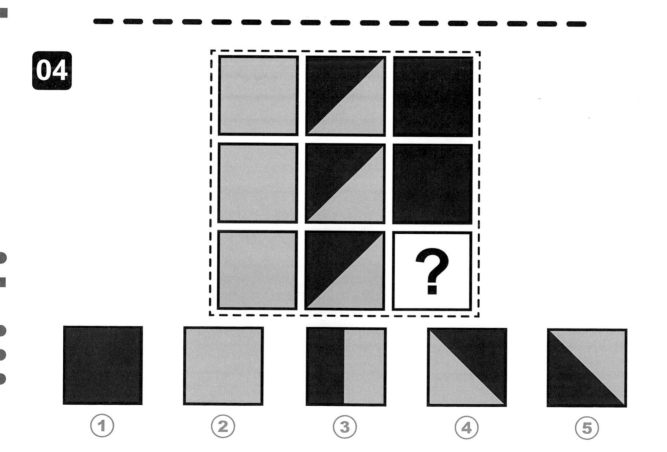

① ② ③ ④ ⑤

05

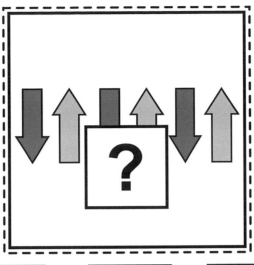

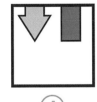  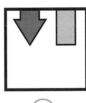 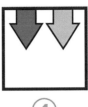 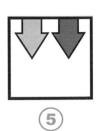

(1)　　　(2)　　　(3)　　　(4)　　　(5)

06

(1)　　　(2)　　　(3)　　　(4)　　　(5)

07

① ② ③ ④ ⑤

08

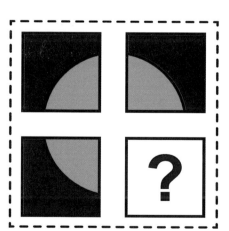

① ② ③ ④ ⑤

NNAT®2 – Level D

09

① ② ③ ④ ⑤

10

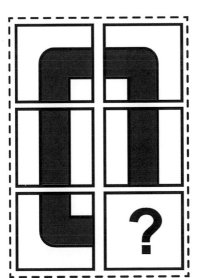

 ①  ②  ③ ④  ⑤

11

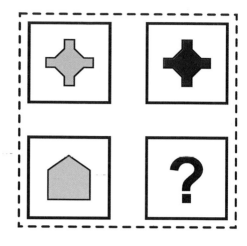

① ② ③ ④ ⑤

12

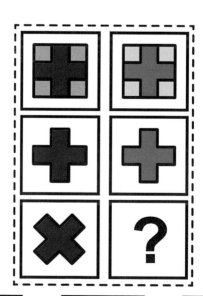

① ② ③ ④ ⑤

13

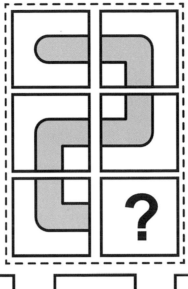

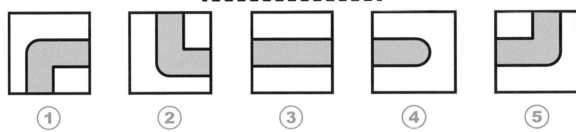

① ② ③ ④ ⑤

14

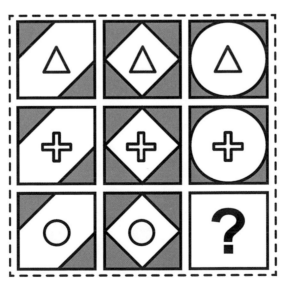

   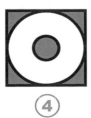 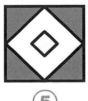

① ② ③ ④ ⑤

15

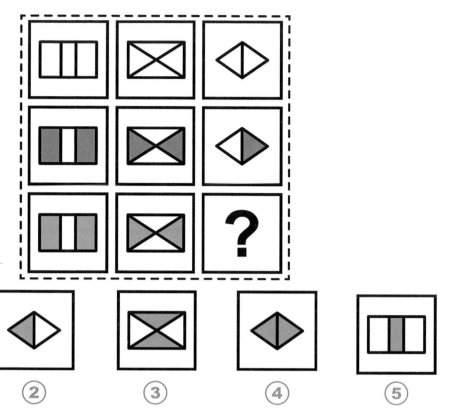

16

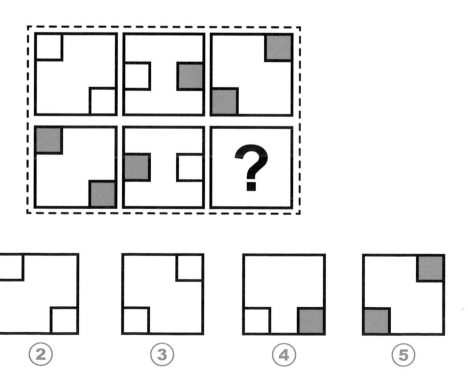

NNAT®2 – Level D   Bright Kids NYC Inc ©

17

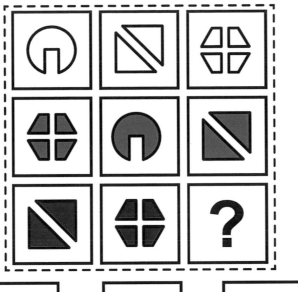

① ② ③ ④ ⑤

18

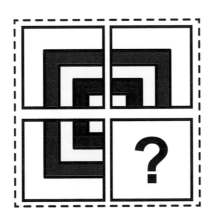

① ② ③ ④ ⑤

19

① ② ③ ④ ⑤

20

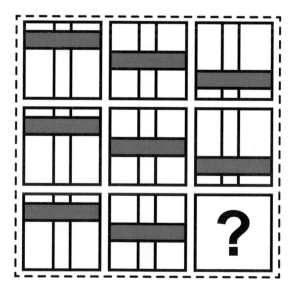

  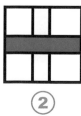 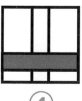

① ② ③ ④ ⑤

NNAT®2 – Level D

21

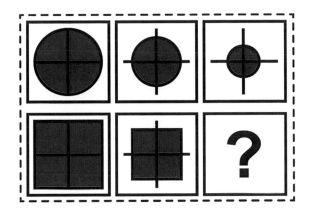

   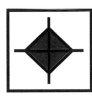 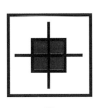

① ② ③ ④ ⑤

- - - - - - - - - - -

22

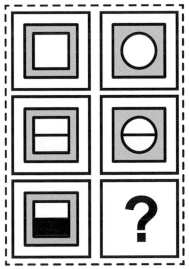

① ② ③ ④ ⑤

23

    ①   ②   ③   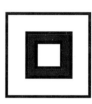 ④   ⑤

24

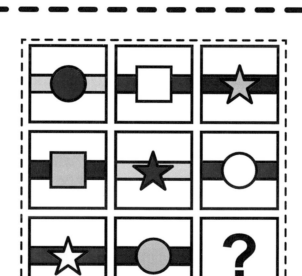

 ①   ②   ③   ④   ⑤

25

① ② ③ ④ ⑤

26

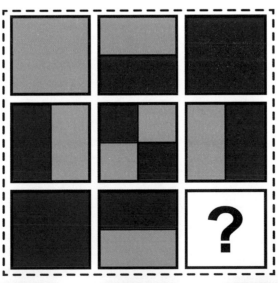

① ② ③ ④ ⑤

27

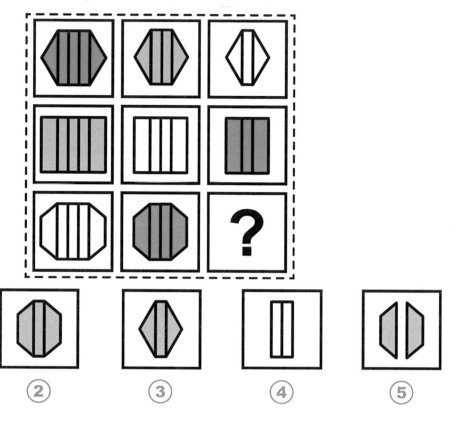

① ② ③ ④ ⑤

28

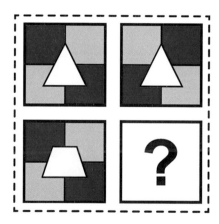

① ② ③ ④ ⑤

29

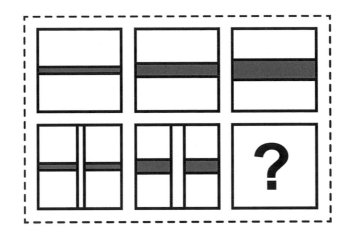

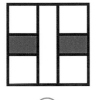 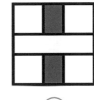 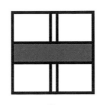 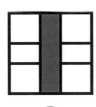 

① ② ③ ④ ⑤

30

① ② ③ ④ ⑤

31

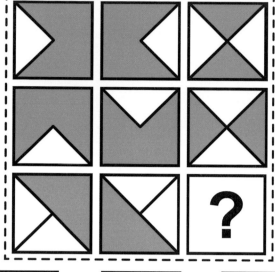

    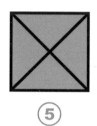

①   ②   ③   ④   ⑤

32

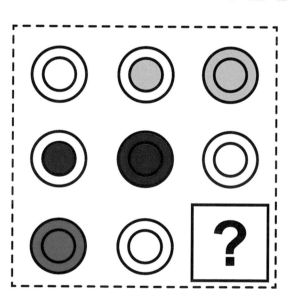

  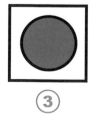  

①   ②   ③   ④   ⑤

    NNAT®2 – Level D   Bright Kids NYC Inc ©

33

① ② ③ ④ ⑤

34

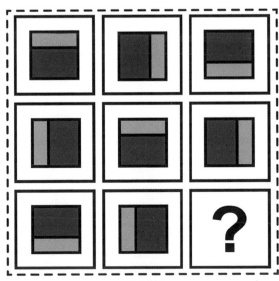

① ② ③ ④ ⑤

35

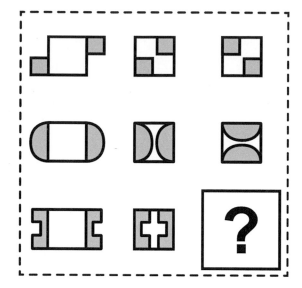

① ② ③ ④ ⑤

36

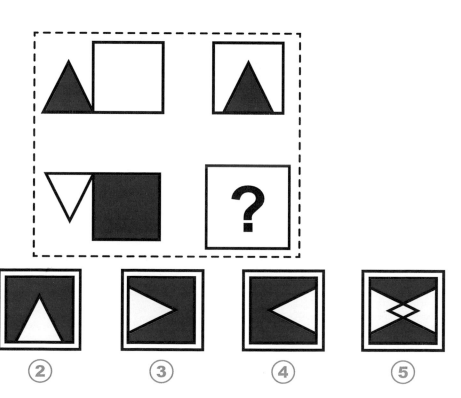

① ② ③ ④ ⑤

NNAT®2 – Level D Bright Kids NYC Inc ©

37

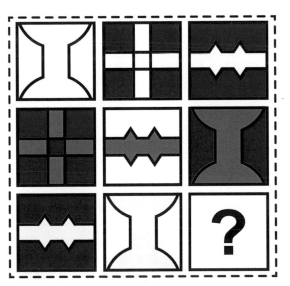

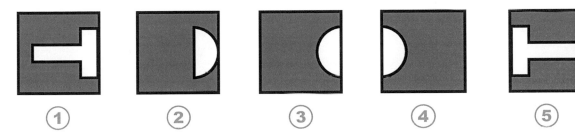

① ② ③ ④ ⑤

38

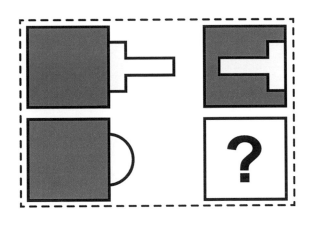

 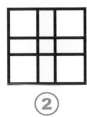  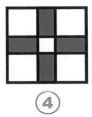

① ② ③ ④ ⑤

39

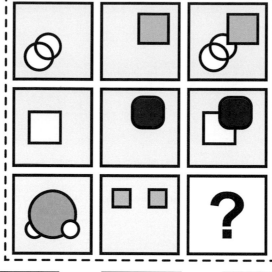

① ② ③ ④ ⑤

40

① ② ③ ④ ⑤

41

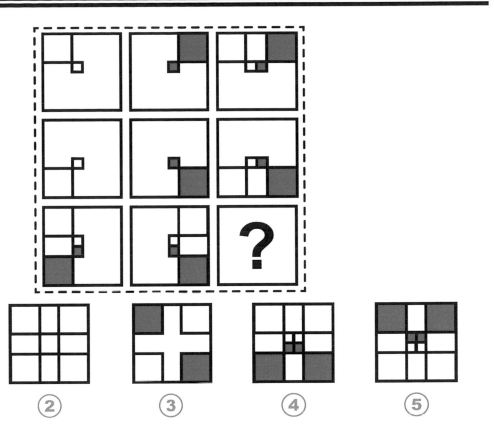

① ② ③ ④ ⑤

42

① ② ③ ④ ⑤

43

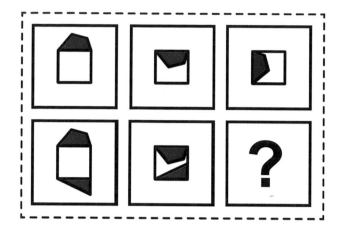

① ② ③ ④ ⑤

44

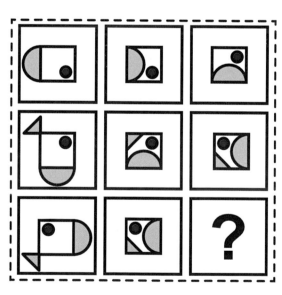

① ② ③ ④ ⑤

NNAT®2 – Level D

45

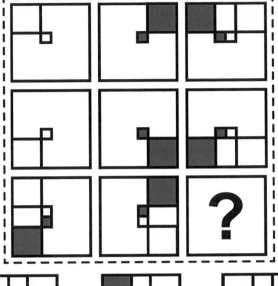

① ② ③ ④ ⑤

46

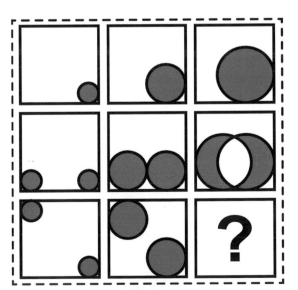

① ② ③ ④ ⑤

47

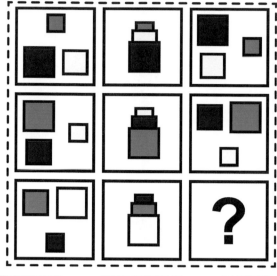

①

②

③

④

⑤

48

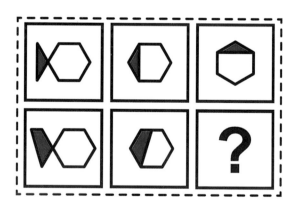

①   ②   ③   ④   ⑤

NNAT®2 – Level D

Bright Kids NYC
NNAT®2 Practice Test

Additional Challenges

NNAT®2 – Level D   Bright Kids NYC Inc ©

01

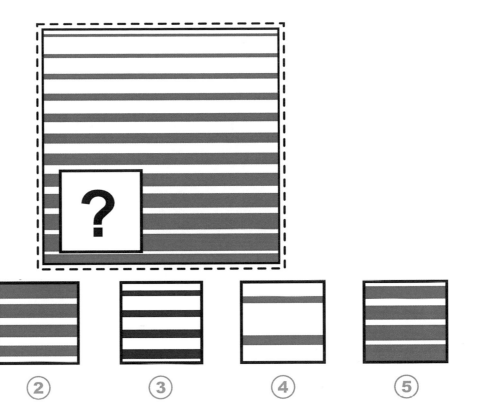

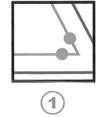
① ② ③ ④ ⑤

02

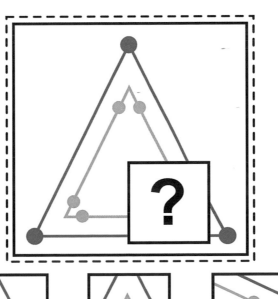

① ② ③ ④ ⑤

03

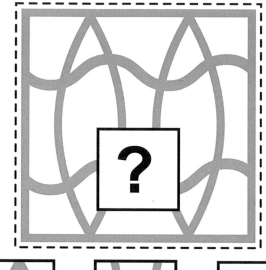

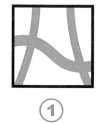  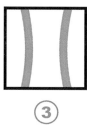 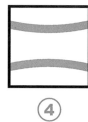 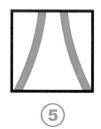

① ② ③ ④ ⑤

04

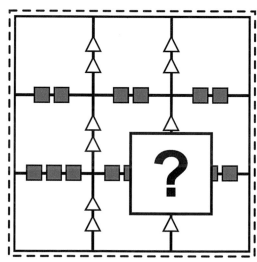

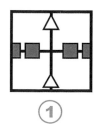 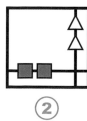 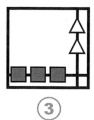 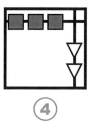 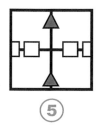

① ② ③ ④ ⑤

NNAT®2 – Level D

05

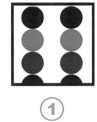  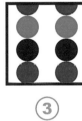 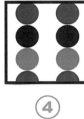 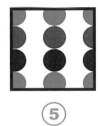

① ② ③ ④ ⑤

06

   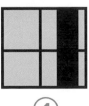 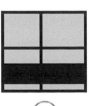

① ② ③ ④ ⑤

07

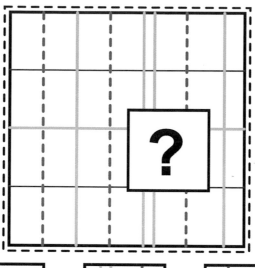

    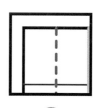

① ② ③ ④ ⑤

08

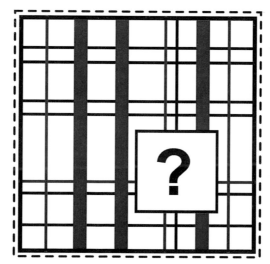

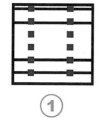    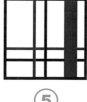

① ② ③ ④ ⑤

09

① ② ③ ④ ⑤

10

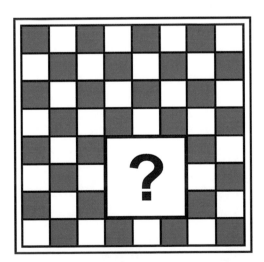

 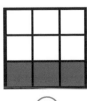 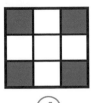 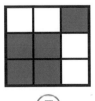

① ② ③ ④ ⑤

NNAT®2 – Level D

Answer Keys

NNAT®2 – Level D

Answer Key - Level D

	Correct Answer	Child's Answer
S1	4	
S2	1	
S3	1	
1.	4	
2.	5	
3.	2	
4.	1	
5.	3	
6.	2	
7.	2	
8.	5	
9.	5	
10.	3	
11.	5	
12.	5	
13.	4	
14.	3	
15.	1	
16.	3	
17.	4	
18.	1	
19.	5	
20.	4	
21.	5	
22.	1	
23.	3	

	Correct Answer	Child's Answer
24.	3	
25.	2	
26.	2	
27.	2	
28.	4	
29.	1	
30.	1	
31.	4	
32.	5	
33.	1	
34.	1	
35.	3	
36.	1	
37.	3	
38.	3	
39.	5	
40.	2	
41.	4	
42.	1	
43.	4	
44.	3	
45.	1	
46.	1	
47.	2	
48.	4	

Answer Key - Additional Challenges

	Correct Answer	Child's Answer
1.	5	
2.	1	
3.	1	
4.	1	
5.	4	
6.	5	
7.	3	
8.	5	
9.	1	
10.	3	